Progress with Oxford

Age 3-4

Phonics

Hello! I'm Bub.

Hello! I'm Hub.

Contents

Key

 Say the sound

 Circle

 Draw

 Colour

 Match

 Play together

 Find the sticker

OXFORD
UNIVERSITY PRESS

The s sound

 Say the **s** sound.

 Circle the pictures that **start with** the **s** sound.

 **Super!**

 Circle the pictures that **contain** the **s** sound.

 **Think of other words that start with S.**

  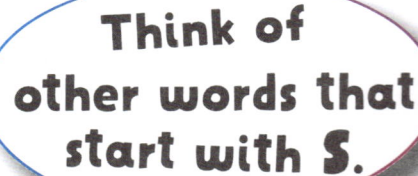

 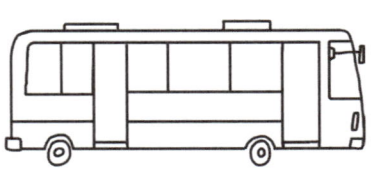

 **Play with sounds**

Be a super-spotter. Find things that start with the **s** sound then say, for example, 'I am a super-spotter! Sofa!'

The a sound

 Say the **a** sound.

 Draw a 😊 next to the pictures that **start with** the **a** sound.

  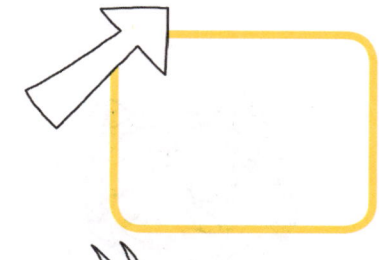

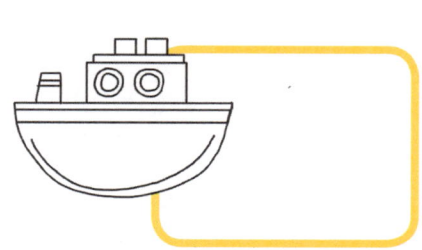 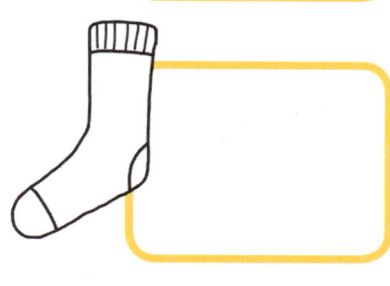 

 Draw a 😊 next to the pictures that **contain** the **a** sound.

 Colour the **amazing** acrobatic ant.

Talk about names that start with the **a** sound for the ant.

The t sound

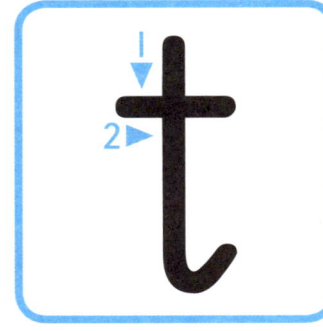

 Say the **t** sound.

 Colour the pictures that **start with** the **t** sound.

Well done!

 Circle the pictures that **contain** the **t** sound.

Give yourself a sticker

 Play with sounds

How fast can you say this tongue-twister?
Ten tigers tickled Timmy tortoise.

Now – track how you're doing on page 32!

The p sound

 Say the **p** sound.

 Circle the pictures that **start with** the **p** sound.

  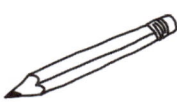 

 Circle the pictures that **contain** the **p** sound.

   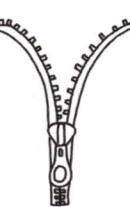

 Draw some foods on the panda's plate that **start with** or **contain** the **p** sound.

Peas, pineapple, pizza, pie, spaghetti, apple.

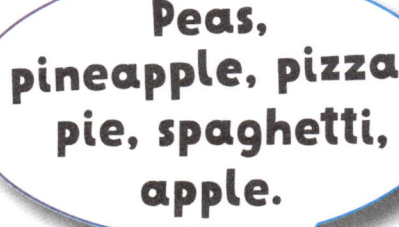

The i sound

 Say the **i** sound.

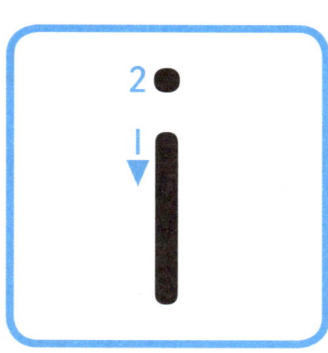

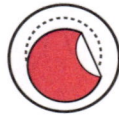 Put an iguana sticker next to the picture that **starts with** the **i** sound.

    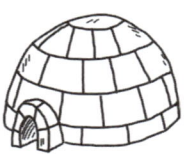 

 Put an iguana sticker next to the picture that **contains** the **i** sound.

 Draw an iguana in the igloo.

Interesting!

Talk about names that start with the **i** sound for the iguana.

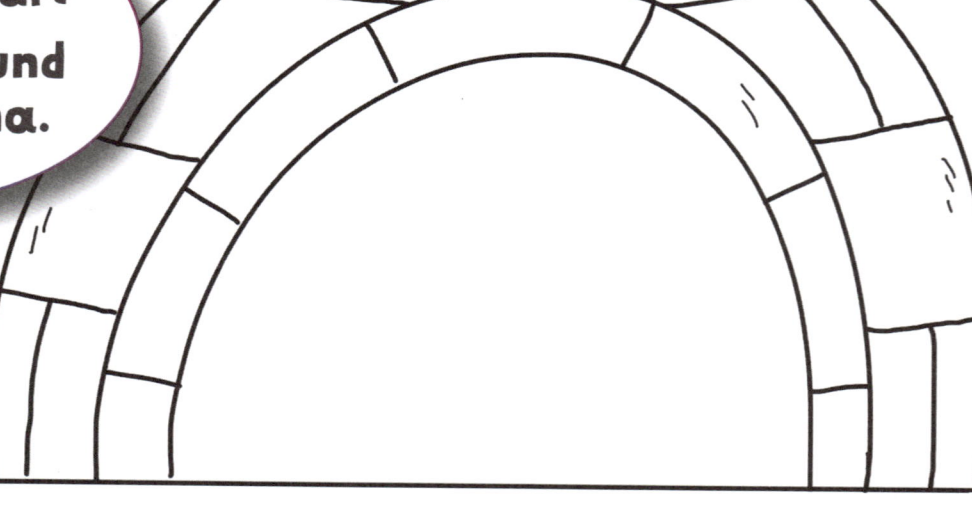

The n sound

 Say the **n** sound.

 Colour the pictures that **start with** the **n** sound.

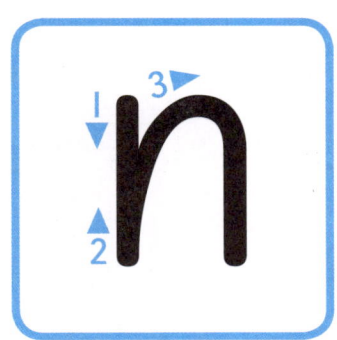

 ★★ Circle the pictures that **contain** the **n** sound.

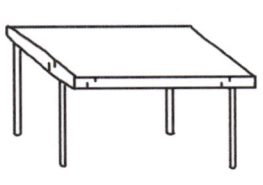

Well done!

 Play with sounds

Play a memory game. Close your eyes then name two things on the page that start with the **n** sound.

Give yourself a sticker

7

Now – track how you're doing on page 32!

s, a, t, p, i and n

 Say the sounds: **s a t p i n**

 Match the pictures that **start with** the same sounds.

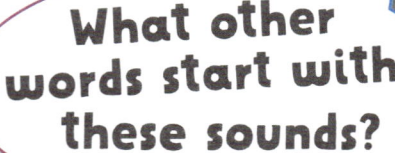
What other words start with these sounds?

Read the word and circle the matching picture.

You can read!

 p i n

Give yourself a sticker

Now – track how you're doing on page 32!

The m sound

 Say the **m** sound.

 Draw a mouth on the monsters next to the pictures that **start with** the **m** sound.

Marvellous monsters!

 Draw a mouth on the monster next to the picture that **contains** the **m** sound.

 Colour this messy monster munching muffins.

Talk about names that start with the **m** sound for the monster.

The d sound

 Say the **d** sound.

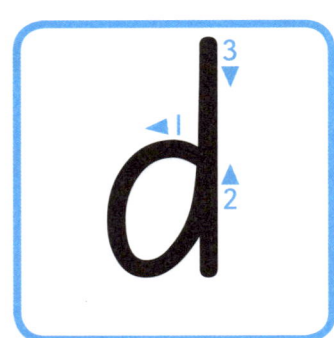

 Draw a daisy next to the pictures that **start with** the **d** sound.

 Draw a daisy next to the pictures that **contain** the **d** sound.

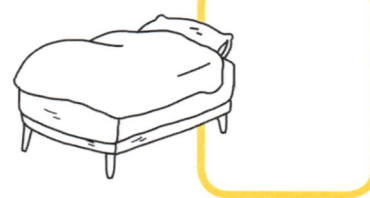

 Draw dots on the dinosaur.

Talk about names that start with the **d** sound for the dinosaur.

The g sound

 Say the **g** sound.

 Colour the pictures that **start with** the **g** sound.

 Colour the pictures that **contain** the **g** sound.

 Draw gloves and glasses on Gus Gorilla.

Give yourself a sticker

The o sound

 Say the **o** sound.

 Circle the pictures that **start with** the **o** sound.

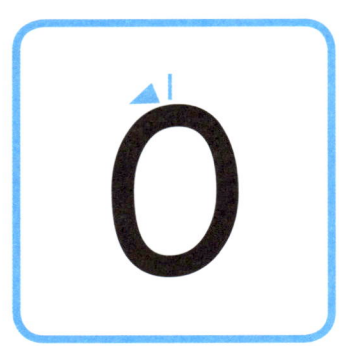

 Colour the pictures that **contain** the **o** sound.

 **Play with sounds**

Draw a big **o** in the air in front of you, then jump through it and shout out the **o** sound.

Remember: start at the top and circle to the left.

The c sound

 Say the **c** sound.

 Put a cat sticker next to the pictures that **start with** the **c** sound.

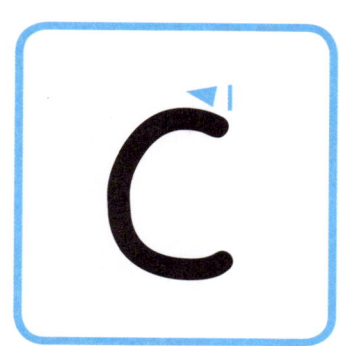

 Carefully colour this curly caterpillar.

Talk about foods that start with the **c** sound to give to the caterpillar.

Cool caterpillar!

The k sound

 Say the **k** sound.

 Colour the pictures that **start with** the **k** sound.

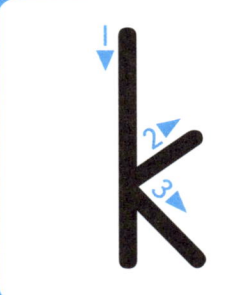

Listen – cat, koala. The **k** sounds like **C**!

 Colour the pictures that **contain** the **k** sound.

 Draw a crown on King Koala.

Give yourself a sticker

Now – track how you're doing on page 32!

m, d, g, o, c and k

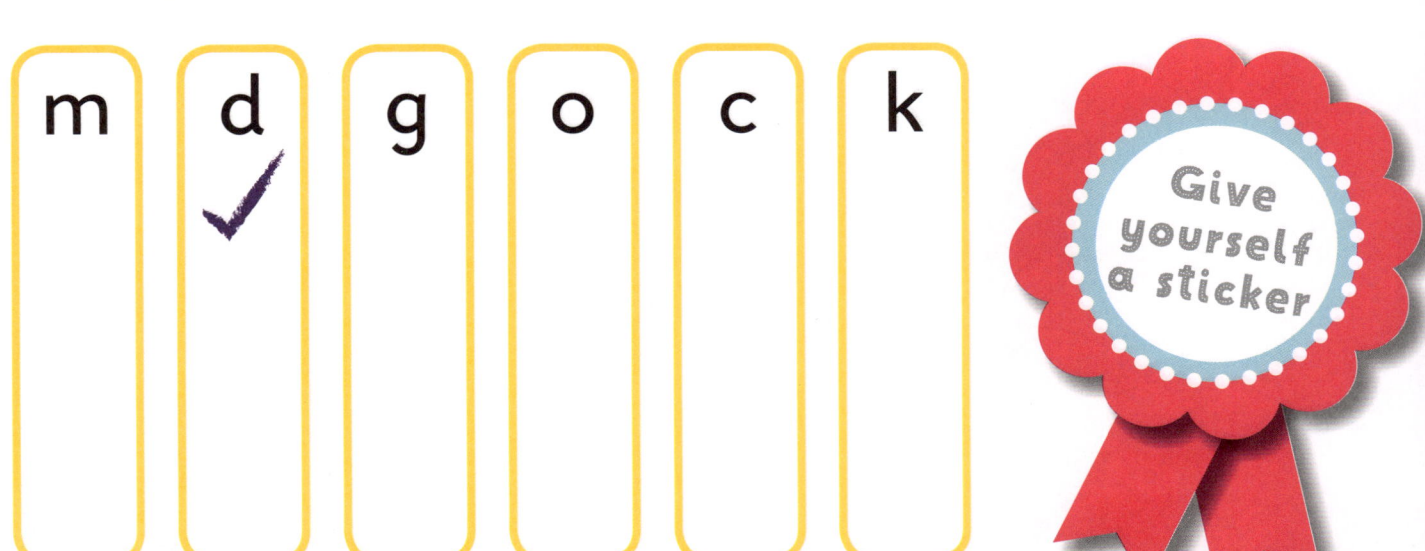

Say the sounds: **m d g o c k**

Look at the picture. Tick the letters every time you find a word that starts with that sound.

m	d	g	o	c	k
	✔				

Give yourself a sticker

Now – track how you're doing on page 32!

The e sound

 Say the **e** sound.

 Circle the pictures that **start with** the **e** sound.

 Circle the pictures that **contain** the **e** sound.

 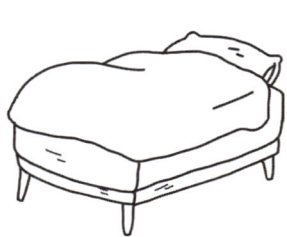  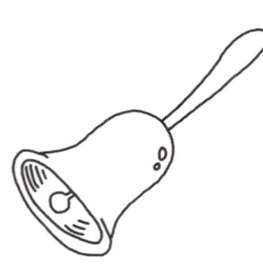

 Read the word and circle the matching picture.

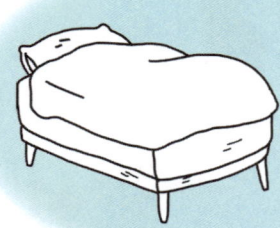 <u>b e d</u>

I love my bed!

16

Stickers for page 6

Stickers for page 13

Stickers for page 31

s a t p i n

m d g o c k

e u r h b f

l j v w y z

Stickers for page 19

Reward Stickers

Character stickers

The u sound

 Say the **u** sound.

 Colour the objects under the umbrella if they **contain** the **u** sound.

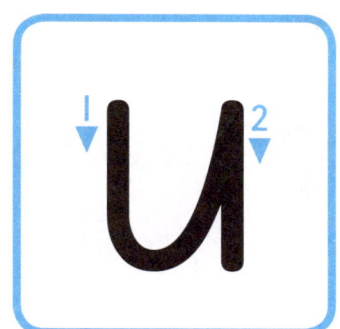

It is fun under the umbrella!

 Draw you and your friends on the bus.

Us on the bus!

The r sound

 Say the **r** sound.

 Draw a ring under the pictures that **start with** the **r** sound.

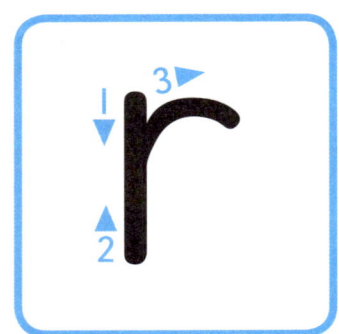

 Draw a ring under the pictures that **contain** the **r** sound.

 Draw a really racy red rocket!

Give yourself a sticker

Now – track how you're doing on page 32!

The h sound

 Say the **h** sound.

 Put a hamster sticker next to the pictures that **start with** the **h** sound.

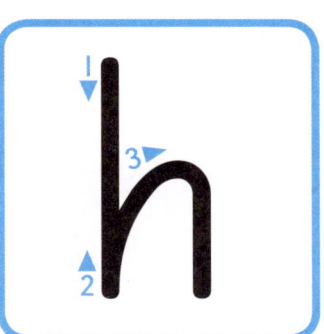

 Draw a house for a happy hamster.

A happy hamster!

The b sound

 Say the **b** sound.

 Colour the boxes next to the pictures that **start with** the **b** sound.

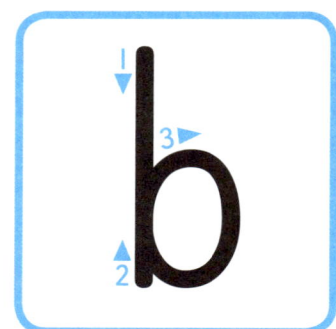

 Colour the boxes next to the pictures that **contain** the **b** sound.

 Make this butterfly beautiful.

That is a brilliant, big and beautiful butterfly!

The f sound

 Say the **f** sound.

 Colour the flowers next to the pictures that **start with** the **f** sound.

Fantastic flowers!

 Colour the flowers next to the pictures that **contain** the **f** sound.

Give yourself a sticker

Play with sounds

Count to ten. Every time you say the **f** sound, hold up a finger.

How many fingers are you holding up?

Now – track how you're doing on page 32!

e, u, r, h, b and f

 Say one of these sounds: **e u r h b f**.

 Choose a colour and colour the pictures that **start with** the sound you chose.

I will colour the pictures that start with the **r** sound red.

 Choose another sound and colour the pictures that begin with it.

 Match the pictures that **start with** the same sounds.

Give yourself a sticker

Now – track how you're doing on page 32!

The l sound

 Say the l sound.

 Colour the lollipops next to the pictures that **start with** the l sound.

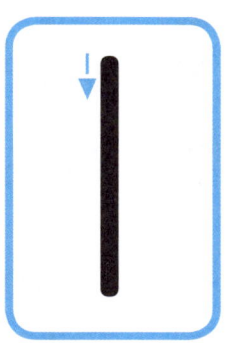

 Colour the lollipops next to the pictures that **contain** the l sound.

 Look! Lots of little lorries. Colour them in.

Talk about things that start with the l sound that might be in the lorries.

The j sound

 Say the j sound.

 Circle the pictures that **start with** the j sound.

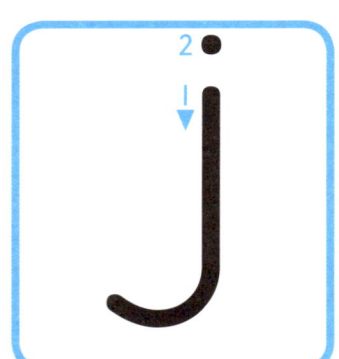

 Circle the pictures that **contain** the j sound.

 **Play with sounds**

Play Jumping Js. Every time you say a word that starts with the j sound, jump forward. Try to jump across the whole room with different words.

What else begins with j?

The v sound

 Say the **v** sound.

 Colour the pictures that **start with** the **v** sound.

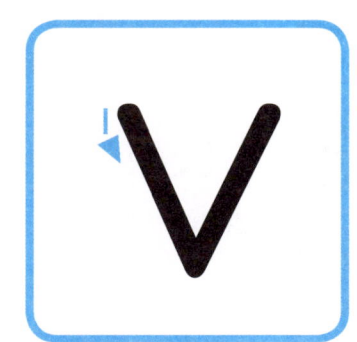

 Colour the pictures that **contain** the **v** sound.

 ★★ Circle the heaviest person.

Vinnie Viking is **very** heavy.

Val Vet

Vinnie Viking

Give yourself a sticker

The w sound

 Say the **w** sound.

 Colour the wands next to the pictures that **start with** the **w** sound.

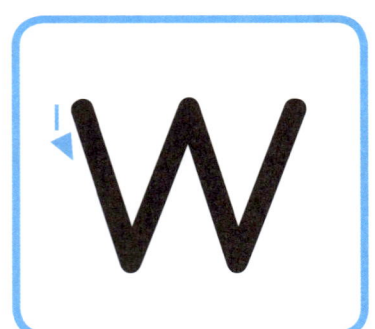

 Colour the wands next to the pictures that **contain** the **w** sound.

 Colour the wonderful wiggling worm.

Wow!

26

The y sound

 Say the **y** sound.

 Circle the pictures that **start with** the **y** sound.

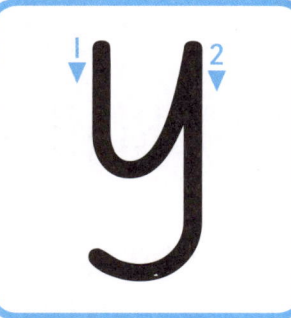

Yippee!

 **Play with sounds**

Play Yes! Yellow! Hunt for yellow things. When you find one, say, for example, 'Yes! Yellow cup!'

I love playing games, do you?

The z sound

 Say the **z** sound.

 Draw a zigzag next to the pictures that **start with** the **z** sound.

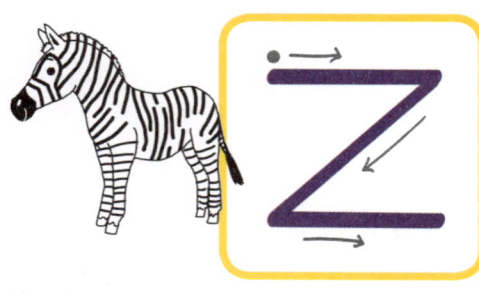

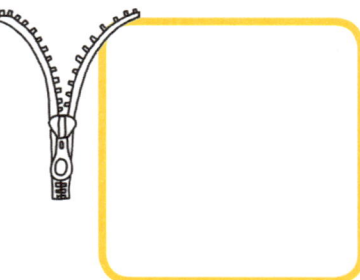

 Draw a zigzag next to the picture that **contains** the **z** sound.

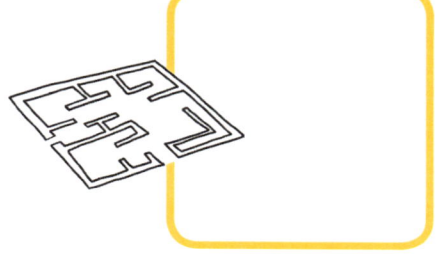

 Follow the maze to help Zelda Zebra find her food.

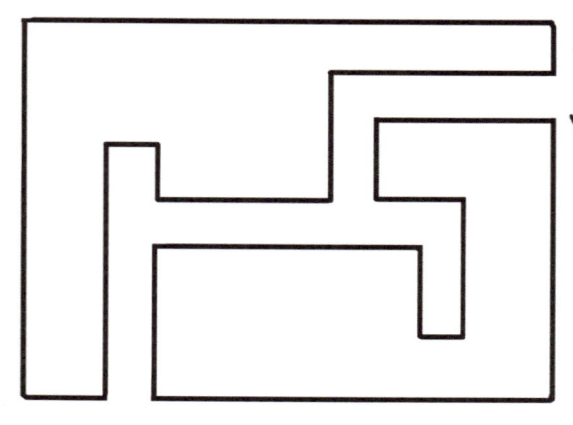

Give yourself a sticker

Now – track how you're doing on page 32!

l, j, v, w, y and z

 Say the sounds: l j v w y z

 Match the pictures that **start with** the same letter sounds.

 Can you **remember** your **sounds**?

 Play with sounds.

Choose a sound. Close your eyes and name as many things as you can remember from the page that start with that sound. Do it again with another sound.

 Give yourself a sticker

Now – track how you're doing on page 32!

Revise!

Look at the picture. When you find something on the picture that starts with the sound, put a sticker next to the letter.

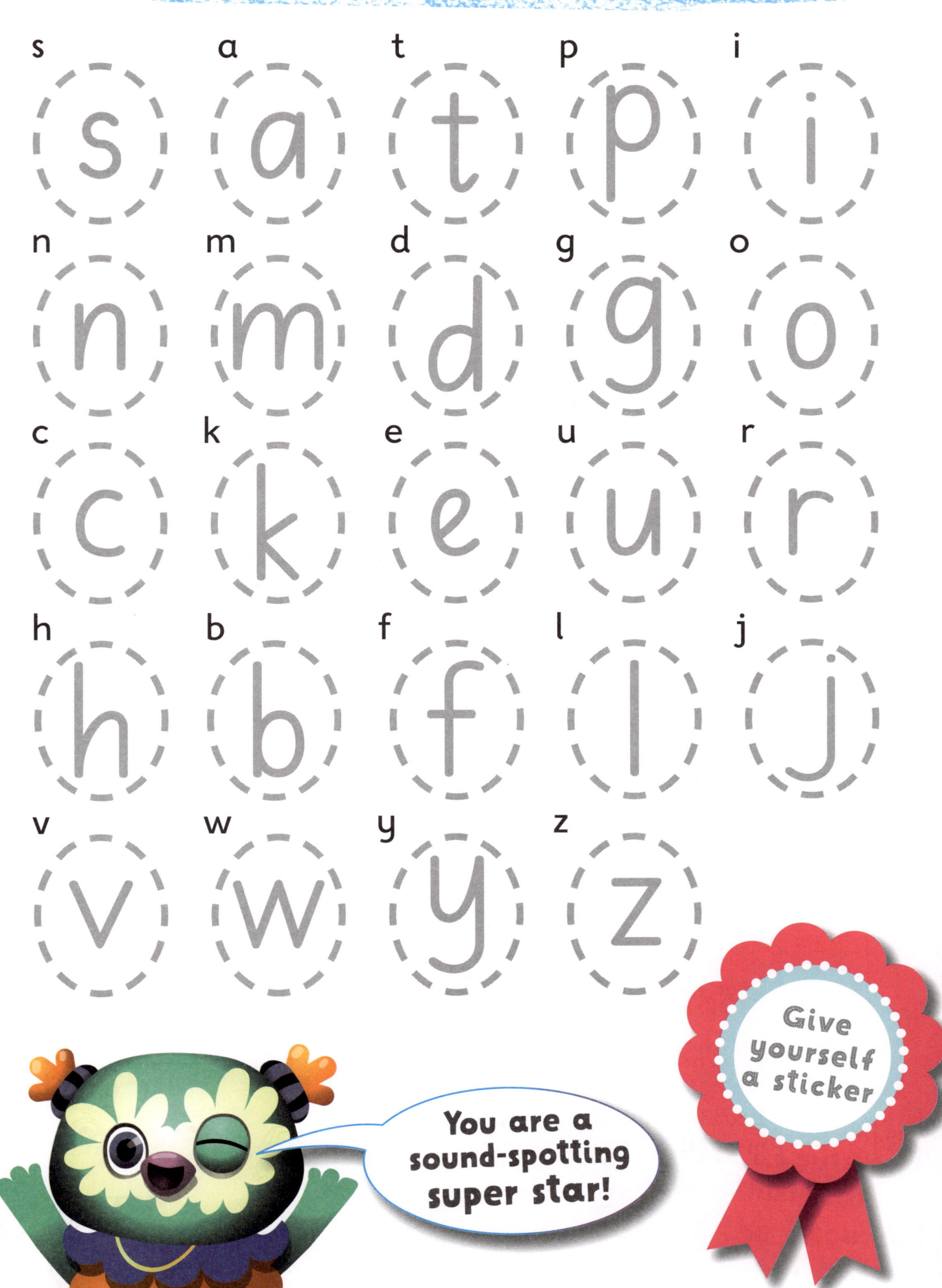

s　　a　　t　　p　　i

n　　m　　d　　g　　o

c　　k　　e　　u　　r

h　　b　　f　　l　　j

v　　w　　y　　z

You are a
sound-spotting
super star!

Give
yourself
a sticker

Now – track how you're doing on page 32!

Progress Chart

Colour in a face.

😊 I can do this well

😐 I can do this but need more practice

☹ I find this difficult

Page	I Can . . .	How did you do?		
2–4	I can hear the sounds s, a and t in words.	😊	😐	☹
5–7	I can hear the sounds p, i and n in words.	😊	😐	☹
8	I can hear the sounds s, a, t, p, i and n in words.	😊	😐	☹
9–11	I can hear the sounds m, d and g in words.	😊	😐	☹
12–14	I can hear the sounds o, c and k in words.	😊	😐	☹
15	I can hear the sounds m, d, g, o, c and k in words.	😊	😐	☹
16–18	I can hear the sounds e, u and r in words.	😊	😐	☹
19–21	I can hear the sounds h, b and f in words.	😊	😐	☹
22	I can hear the sounds e, u, r, h, b and f in words.	😊	😐	☹
23–25	I can hear the sounds l, j and v in words.	😊	😐	☹
26–28	I can hear the sounds w, y and z in words.	😊	😐	☹
29	I can hear the sounds l, j, v, w, y and z in words.	😊	😐	☹
30–31	I can hear all the letter sounds in this book in words.	😊	😐	☹

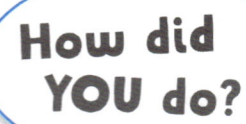

How did YOU do?